ANCIENT ROME

ANCIENT ROME

by David and Bridget Trump

Illustrated by Francis Phillipps

GRANADA
London Toronto Sydney New York

The frontispiece shows the remains of the forum, a collection of public buildings at the heart of Rome.

Granada Publishing Limited
Frogmore, St Albans, Herts AL2 2NF
and
36 Golden Square, London W1R 4AH
866 United Nations Plaza, New York, NY 10017, USA
117 York Street, Sydney, NSW 2000, Australia
100 Skyway Avenue, Rexdale, Ontario, M9W 3A6, Canada
61 Beach Road, Auckland, New Zealand

Published by Granada Publishing 1982

Copyright © Granada

British Library Cataloguing in Publication Data

Trump, David
Ancient Rome. – (Granada guide series; 19)
1. Rome – Civilization – Juvenile literature
I. Title   II. Trump, Bridget
937   DG77

ISBN 0 246 11797 4

Designed and edited by Holland & Clark Ltd.

Printed and bound in Great Britain by
William Collins Sons & Co Ltd, Glasgow

Contents

Who Were the Romans?   6

Everyday Life   16

Roman Religion   26

Roman Achievements   36

The Army and Navy   46

Roman Emperors   54

Index   62

Who Were the Romans?

The first Romans lived in small oval huts on hills beside the River Tiber. Because roads up and down Italy crossed the river here, Rome was a good place for traders, and the Romans became rich and powerful enough to conquer local tribes. Because of its prosperity and sound government, other tribes were not too unwilling to become part of the Roman state. Next, the Romans took over cities in southern Italy which the Greeks had founded. These cities were very luxurious, but unable to defend themselves against Rome's well disciplined army.

This is how a dwelling built by the first Romans in the 8th century BC would have looked. The thatched roof was held up by wooden posts and the walls were plastered with mud. It was about 4 metres long.

Once the Romans controlled Italy, they wanted Sicily, the big island to the south-west. Part of this belonged to the Carthaginians, who had set up trading stations around the west Mediterranean. The Romans had to build ships in order to defeat the Carthaginians.

The city states of Greece were weak and divided, and the Celtic tribes of France and Germany, though much more warlike, were no more able to unite. So by 31 BC the Romans ruled a vast area.

Latins and Etruscans

The area around Rome was known as Latium and its inhabitants spoke the Latin language. (No-one speaks Latin now, but it is the basis of many European languages, particularly Italian.) The Romans believed that their city had been founded by Romulus and Remus, twin brothers abandoned by their mother and raised by a she-wolf. The city took its name from Romulus who is said to have become the first king of Rome in 753 BC, after killing his brother. This date fits in well with the age given by archaeologists to the earliest known remains of the city – some huts found on one of the hills.

Romulus and Remus founded Rome in 753 BC. According to a legend they were reared by a she-wolf. This coin was minted in the 3rd century BC.

Romulus was followed by six other kings. We know nothing about the first three, but the fourth, Tarquinius Priscus, was an Etruscan, from Etruria in northern Italy. The Etruscans were a highly civilized people who were powerful in the sixth century BC. In many ways their culture was similar to that of the Greeks; they were energetic and practical, they were skilled metal-workers and, with the help of their horses and chariots, they were good fighters. The Etruscans changed Rome from a village of mud huts to a walled city with stone buildings. But they became unpopular, and the last king, Tarquin the Proud, was driven out by his Latin subjects in 509 BC.

The Republic

Once Tarquin had been driven out, the very word *rex*, king, was hated by the Romans. The Etruscans did try to get control of Rome again, and the story of Horatius keeping the bridge describes how one such attempt was foiled. The Romans had to create a new form of government for themselves. They called it a republic. The big difference was that instead of one man being king for life, they elected two consuls who held power for just one year. The consuls shared the jobs of commander-in-chief of the army and head of state, and there were a number of other magistrates to collect taxes and run the law courts. The kings had also carried out religious duties, and these were taken over by priests. The chief priest was called the Pontifex Maximus.

The Etruscans liked hunting and fishing. They left the Romans with similar tastes, as can be seen in these scenes from a mosaic.

Roman society was split into two main classes, the patricians, the top people, and the plebeians. Patrician power was centred in the Senate, a council of men from the most important families. Throughout the Republic there was a struggle by the plebeians for greater equality with the patricians. Their first success was being allowed an Assembly, whose decisions were influential but not as powerful as those of the Senate.

The plebeians won the right to marry patricians, and later to become consuls. They also created two special officials of their own called tribunes to look after the welfare of the common people. The two tribunes could not make laws, but they could prevent them by saying *veto*, meaning I forbid.

Growth of the Empire

Although Roman power spread quickly throughout Italy, not everyone was happy to be conquered. The Carthaginians who had traded and settled in Sicily and Sardinia fought back. Their brilliant general Hannibal crossed the Alps with his war elephants and almost beat the Roman army.

The Republic could not cope with such emergencies, so one man was appointed dictator. He could give orders to everyone, even the consuls, but once the crisis was over he had to give up his powers. On this occasion, a man known as Fabius Cunctator (the Delayer) was appointed. And, with his cautious tactics, the Romans were eventually victorious.

The letters SPQR stand for Senatus Populusque Romanus – *the Senate and People of Rome. The letters are proudly displayed in stone on many state buildings.*

The Senate (left) was a council of about 300 rich and powerful men. Only they were allowed a broad purple stripe on their white togas. They decided on war or peace and passed new laws. Two consuls, who held supreme power for one year, were elected by the senators. Meetings were held in temples or other large buildings.

The Roman fleet went on to attack the Carthaginians in Spain and in North Africa, where Hannibal was finally defeated at the battle of Zama. Carthage was stripped of power and wealth and in 146 BC was completely destroyed.

Rome had become an empire. Wealth poured into the capital, making the rich richer, but the poor poorer. Different leaders fought each other, causing much misery. None of them was able to hold on to power for long, not even the self-styled emperor Julius Caesar.

Hannibal (right) marched his army all the way from Spain to Italy. He won three great battles but Carthage lost the war.

When a victorious general was allowed by the Senate to hold a triumph (below), he drove through the streets with his soldiers and the prisoners and booty they had captured.

The City

Because Rome grew up gradually over a long period, its streets were not laid out in the tidy grid pattern you see in later Roman towns. Instead they ran in all directions and most were so narrow that two carts could not pass each other. The old part of present day Rome is still much the same.

The city was full of huge public buildings, baths, theatres and shopping arcades. Tourists from all over the empire poured in to see it, just as they do today. One of the biggest attractions was the Colosseum, an amphitheatre in which 70,000 people could sit to

Rome is this shape (above) because of the river and the seven hills on which it is built. The main roads lead out through gates in the walls.

The triumphal arch (right) was put up by the emperor Constantine to commemorate his victories. It is still standing in Rome today.

watch fights between wild beasts or gladiators. Even more people could watch the chariot races in the Circus Maximus, which had a U-shaped track over a kilometre long, with a central barrier on which stood statues and obelisks.

The heart of the city was the Forum Romanum, an open space for public meetings. In the middle of it stood the *rostra*, a platform from which speeches were made. All around were temples and triumphal arches in gleaming marble with gilded statues. The biggest temple was that of the god Jupiter on top of the Capitoline hill.

Everyday Life

Life and religion were closely bound together in Ancient Rome. When a baby was born, offerings of food were made to the gods. If he was a boy – and a patrician – a lucky charm called a *bulla* was put round his neck. As soon as he could walk he was given a white toga with a purple stripe around the edge. The toga was the usual Roman garment for a man, even though it must have been heavy and awkward to wear. It was made of woollen cloth in the shape of a half circle six metres across. Poorer people wore grey togas.

Rich Romans lived in palatial villas built around a courtyard. Slaves cooked, carried and cleaned. Poorer people lived in cramped flats with few luxuries.

A small pottery lamp. It burned olive oil and the wick came out of the spout.

This doll is made of bone with peg joints. The face was painted.

Modestina had this bone comb specially made for her. It has her name on it.

When a boy was sixteen he 'came of age' and put aside his bulla and striped toga. His first beard hairs were put in a box and dedicated to the gods. All high-class Romans were clean-shaven. Men were shaved by personal slaves or by barbers.

A boy might be sent to a small school, or have a private tutor. The first tutor was called a *litterator*, then came a *grammaticus*, and lastly a *rhetor* to teach public speaking. Educated Romans knew Greek as well as Latin. Most teachers were Greek, and other Greeks worked as artists and secretaries in Italy.

Only girls from rich families were educated. Girls could be married at the age of twelve. Their marriages were arranged by the head of the family, the *pater familias*, usually the grandfather. The couple clasped hands in a simple ceremony. Divorce was easy for both men and women. Patrician women had their own property and appeared in public with men.

Town Life

The rich lived in great style and comfort, waited on by slaves. Their main meal was in the evening. They lay on couches to eat, propped on their left elbows. The food was cooked over charcoal braziers, using a great deal of olive oil. The rich ate meat every day, with tasty sauces, while the poor made do with bread, cheese, vegetables and porridge.

Shops and workshops opened on to the narrow crowded streets, while people lived in flats above. Houses were built of brick.

Large houses had no outside windows, but were built round open courtyards. This kept them cool in summer and shut out some of the noise from the streets. The houses had central heating, running water and drains. The poor lived in blocks of flats up to five storeys high owned by rich landlords. Clean water had to be carried upstairs from public fountains, and dirty water was simply thrown into the street.

Industry was mostly carried out in small workshops. Only pottery and cloth were produced on a large scale. Most of the work was done by slaves, for even running a business was thought undignified for patricians.

A stone quern (above) for grinding corn. The hollow top was turned by men or donkeys pushing wooden bars. The grain was crushed against a fixed lower stone. Machines were simple, as all energy came from human or animal muscles.

Country Life

The early citizens of Rome had been farmers, only going to war when there was not much work to do on the farm. Later on, when Rome had become a great empire with full-time paid soldiers, people liked to look back to the good old days. Virgil, who lived in the time of Augustus, wrote poems in praise of the Italian countryside. Rich Romans had country houses so they could escape from the heat and bustle of the city. Farming, not industry, was the important thing, with countrymen working their own land. So, when greedy landowners bought up the small farms

Part of a big farm, worked by slave labour. The man on horseback is the overseer.

This wooden plough has an iron coulter and ploughshare. It is pulled by two oxen with a wooden yoke across their shoulders.

to make big estates where the work was nearly all done by slaves, there was trouble. Julius Caesar tried to encourage small farms again by giving plots of land to his veterans – retired soldiers.

Farmers grew crops suited to the Mediterranean climate, which has hot summers and mild winters. These crops included vines and olives, as well as corn. Sheep were kept for wool and for milk, which was made into cheese; cattle were kept for milk and meat. Country people grew fruit and vegetables such as apples, figs, carrots and onions, which they sold in the towns. Fish from around the coasts was dried and sent inland, often to be made into a strongly flavoured and highly popular fish paste.

Wine-making was important. The grapes were crushed by men trampling on them in special troughs from which the juice flowed into jars. When the wine had fermented it could be carried in skins or casks, or put into tall earthenware jars with two handles called *amphorae*. The Romans generally drank their wine mixed with water.

Public Baths

If you lived in a town or city you went to the baths regularly, not just to wash but to meet friends and enjoy yourself. Baths were like clubs. The large, imposing buildings were erected at public expense or by emperors wishing to impress their subjects. Most baths were free; at others a nominal charge was made. Only slaves and the very poor stayed away. Mixed bathing was frowned on, so women had to bathe at separate times from men.

The first thing a man would do was join in exercises – weight-lifting, ball-games, boxing or wrestling, with bowls for the less energetic. The idea was to encourage sweating. After that he rubbed olive oil on to his skin and then scraped off oil, sweat and dust with a curved bronze scraper called a strigil. This was followed by a warm bath in a room called the *tepidarium*. Next came the hot *caldarium*, which was like a sauna. After that he returned to the *tepidarium* before cooling off in the cold *frigidarium*.

The water was heated by huge furnaces, stoked with wood. Hot air from these furnaces was also circulated in spaces under the floors. This form of heating, called a hypocaust, was used in ordinary houses too.

Only the enormous baths in Rome or places where there were natural springs had pools big enough to swim in. The rich owners of country villas had smaller-scale baths in their own houses, and there were baths for the soldiers at all permanent forts.

People went to the baths to enjoy themselves. Big baths had bars, shops, lounges, libraries and gardens attached. There was much noise with people laughing, shouting and singing.

Circuses and Sport

Apart from exercising at the baths, sport for Romans meant watching exciting spectacles. Gladiator fights were put on in special amphitheatres like the Colosseum in Rome. They were paid for by emperors or other rich men who wanted to gain favour with the crowds. Gladiators were usually slaves who had run away or committed a crime. They were kept locked in barracks, where they lived and trained. A few free men also chose to fight for the excitement and the chance of fame and fortune if they survived.

Gladiators were armed in various ways. For instance, a *mirmillo* with helmet, sword and shield, fought against a *retiarius*, with only a weighted net and a tunny fisherman's trident. When a man was beaten to the ground, his life would be spared if the emperor gave the thumbs up sign. If it was thumbs down, he was killed and dragged out of the arena. Other fights involved wild animals, specially imported from Africa, or sea battles, when the arena was flooded and galleys charged each other.

A game like hockey must have been played in Roman times to judge by the curved stick this man (left) is holding.

The Romans loved gladiator fights and other scenes of death and bloodshed. Charioteers in the circus were often thrown out at the sharp turns or when wheels fell off during races. The onlookers placed bets on who would win. Winners got big prizes and became popular heroes.

Roman Religion

The Romans took their private religion seriously. Every family had a special spirit called a *genius*. Ancestors were highly respected and portraits of them were kept in shrines in the house.

Public religion was performed by priests. Ordinary people were not allowed inside temples, but there were processions and games for all to join in on public holidays throughout the year. One festival, the Saturnalia, took place in December. It was a week of ceremonies in honour of Saturn. Slaves and masters changed places and there was fun and feasting. We carry on this tradition in our Christmas celebrations.

The Romans worshipped many gods and goddesses – not all of them models of good behaviour. Jupiter was the chief, together with Juno his wife and Minerva, goddess of wisdom and skill. Mars was god

Jupiter was chief of the Roman gods. Originally he was a Latin sky god. In this statue he is holding a thunderbolt in his left hand. Under influence from the Greeks, he came to be thought the same as their chief god Zeus. He represented those virtues the Romans most admired – bravery, justice and honour. They called him Deus Optimus Maximus – Best and Greatest God. The eagle was a symbol both of Jupiter and of Roman power. It was used on the standards of the Roman legions.

Families made offerings every day to the Lares and Penates, the gods of hearth and store, at shrines in their own homes.

of war; Venus goddess of love; Janus god of gateways (statues show him with two faces, so he could look both forward and back). Vesta, goddess of the hearth, had a circular temple inside which was a sacred fire. The fire was kept alight by six Vestal virgins, who were like nuns. It was believed that a terrible disaster would befall Rome if the fire went out. Even an abstract idea, such as Victory or Fortune, was made into a goddess by the Romans. They often changed their beliefs and adopted gods from other countries.

27

The Emperor as God

In the first century BC, nearly everybody believed in Jupiter and the other gods. But then, even though ceremonial worship was carried on as dutifully as ever, many people ceased to believe in the old gods. New ones from the east were greeted with enthusiasm by people wanting more excitement in their religion. But there was still room for something more tangible. Emperor worship filled the gap. It was a way of uniting people of different races and ensuring absolute loyalty to Rome.

It began when Julius Caesar was in the east and saw how the pharaohs were worshipped by their subjects. He may have intended setting up himself and Cleopatra as divine rulers of the Roman Empire, but before he could do this he was murdered. The ordinary people of Rome loved him so much that in their sorrow at his death they declared him a god.

Augustus, who followed Caesar, never claimed to be a god, but as his power increased more and more people hailed him as one while he was still alive, and he did not stop them. Tiberius, who followed Augustus, told his friends he was only mortal, but his subjects worshipped him as a symbol of the power of Rome. The next emperor was Caligula, a most unpleasant young man who insisted that everyone call him god. No-one believed he was, but they pretended to because they feared him. Claudius knew well that he was not divine but during his reign a large and expensive temple dedicated to him was built at Colchester to impress the newly conquered Britons.

The emperor Claudius looks at a statue of himself as a god. See how similar this statue is to the one of Jupiter on page 26.

Christianity

The only people who refused to worship the emperor were the Christians and for this defiance they were thrown to the lions or killed in other unpleasant ways. All they were asked to do was throw a pinch of incense on to the altar fire, but this was against their faith. Like the Jews, Christians believed there was only one true god; all others were merely idols. The Romans had lots of gods themselves, and did not mind what others their subjects worshipped, provided they showed they were loyal citizens by bowing to the image of the emperor. So the Romans could not understand the Christian point of view.

Christians became unpopular because they were

honest, quiet and law-abiding at a time when most people were the opposite. Roman religion set no rules for behaviour, while the eastern gods positively encouraged bad habits.

Jesus Christ was born during the reign of Augustus who established the *Pax Romana* (Roman Peace) all the way from Arabia to Spain. By the time Jesus grew up, Tiberius had become emperor. The man responsible for crucifying Jesus in AD 30 was Pontius Pilate, the Roman governor of Judaea. Crucifixion was a slow, painful way of executing people, used a lot by the Romans, but mainly for slaves. St Paul, who was a citizen of Rome, was beheaded. Christianity spread because it offered hope of a better life after death. Under Constantine it became the official religion of the Empire.

A monogram (above) made from the first two letters of the word Christ in Greek writing.

Catacombs were underground rooms and passages cut in soft rock and used mainly for burials. Funeral services were held in small chapels like this one (left).

31

Eastern Gods

The Romans took over religious ideas and superstitions from all the people with whom they came in contact, starting with the Etruscans. From them the Romans learnt how to 'foretell the future' by watching how birds flew and from the entrails of sacrificial animals. It was as a result of mixing with Greeks living in Italy that the Romans began giving Greek names and characters to their own Latin gods. Then as Roman conquests spread further, particularly eastwards, more and more new gods were introduced to Rome. The first of these was Cybele, the Great Mother, who was brought from Turkey in 204

The woman (above) is a priestess of the Egyptian goddess Isis. In her right hand she holds a sistrum.

BC. The ancient land of Egypt gave the goddess Isis, who brought Osiris back to life.

As part of the worship of Bacchus (Greek Dionysus), god of wine, his followers got very drunk and riotous, so worship of the deity had to be forbidden in Rome. The Persian god Mithras was very different. Only men could take part in his secret rites, and his followers had to be brave and truthful. Mithraism was a complete religion, with Ahura Mazda, god of light and good, and Ahriman, god of darkness and evil. Mithras was believed to have killed a bull, from whose blood all life sprang up.

Mithras was born in a cave, so his temples were made dark and mysterious. The carving shows Mithras killing a bull.

Burial of the Dead

Every Roman wanted as grand a funeral as he could afford. Many people joined clubs to which they paid money during their working lives to cover the cost of their own funerals. Bodies were either buried in the ground or cremated and the ashes put into a special urn. In both cases there were ceremonies and prayers led by a priest. A rich family would hire musicians and women to wail and beat their breasts in the procession. Servants carried wax masks of the dead person's ancestors. The procession halted in the forum and a member of the family made a speech in honour of the dead from the rostra.

It was customary for a man to free some of his slaves in his will. These ex-slaves carried the body on an open bier. The dead man's wife followed behind,

Burials were not allowed inside towns, so the dead were placed in tombs along the roads just outside (left). Peoples' names and ages at death were carved on tombstones (above).

her hair hanging loose, not piled up on her head in the elaborate and constantly changing fashions of the Roman Empire. She was accompanied by relations and clients of the dead man, wearing grey or black togas as a sign of mourning. Clients were middle class citizens who attached themselves to a rich patrician. They crowded round him when he appeared in public and applauded his speeches. In return he gave them food and money. They truly would have been sorry when a generous patron died.

Tombs varied greatly in different parts of the Empire, and also according to what people could afford. In places with only a thin layer of soil, tombs were cut in the rock. Jesus was laid in such a rock-cut tomb.

Roman Achievements

Above all else, the Romans wanted their art to be realistic. Their statues seem almost to breathe and move. Their portraits show every wart and wrinkle. Scenes of soldiers or workmen going about their daily tasks are accurate down to the exact shape of a shield or axe. This makes it possible for us to imagine just what they were like in life. Look long and hard at a statue of some senator, and you really feel you have got to know him. The Greeks liked to paint or sculpt perfect athletes and graceful girls; the Romans wanted to recognize themselves.

When Augustus erected the Altar of Peace, the figures carved in relief on panels round it were

The pictures and patterns of mosaic floors are all made up of small cubes of different coloured stone or glass set in plaster.

Roman sculptors rarely idealized their subjects. They showed them 'warts and all'.

portraits of him and his family. The emperor Trajan wanted everyone to see how successful he and his army had been fighting the Dacians, who lived in what we now call Romania. So he had a column put up in Rome, 40 metres high, with a statue of himself on top and a series of scenes winding round it like an unbroken comic strip 200 metres long. The scenes show us all the things the soldiers did, enabling us to see at a glance what army life was like. Elsewhere, panels on altars and tombs show us shops, bars, workshops and farms, giving us a clear picture of everyday life.

The most perfect records of everyday life and Roman art come from a terrible disaster. When Vesuvius erupted in AD 79, the city of Pompeii was smothered in volcanic ash which preserved almost everything. Beautiful pictures decorating the walls of rooms, paved streets, buildings private and public can all be seen today much as they were before the town was buried.

Architecture and Building

Arches and vaults are the key features of Roman buildings. The Etruscans showed the Romans how to build stone arches. The Romans then went on to use arches not only in buildings like the Colosseum but also for bridges and aqueducts. There used to be eleven aqueducts bringing water into Rome from as far as 80 kilometres away. Keeping water flowing such long distances requires remarkable engineering skills. Joining arches together, the Romans also made vaults that allowed wide spaces to be roofed.

For their buildings the Romans used a lot of bricks and tiles. By mixing gravel, mortar and volcanic ash they also made concrete. Poured into wooden moulds and left to set, this could be made into various shapes, including domes. The Golden House, as Nero's new palace was called, had the first large domes in the world, made from concrete. Walls of such grand buildings were covered with gilding, marble or painted plaster.

When putting up tall buildings, such as this aqueduct (right) the Romans used cranes powered by men in tread-mills.

Temples like these (below), with columns round the outside, copied Greek models. These two stood near the River Tiber in Rome.

Literature

Factual history and light-hearted love poetry are two very different kinds of writing, and yet the Romans excelled at both. Their most famous historian was Livy, who wrote about Rome from its foundation to his own days in the first century BC, and was full of praise for the Romans of the Republic. The next great historian, Tacitus, described the rule of the early emperors, whose lives were full of vice and scandal. Probably they were not quite as bad as Tacitus makes out, though he did his best to be as accurate as possible.

Horace and Catullus wrote love poetry. Catullus's

A Roman library (below); the rolls of papyrus (paper made from a kind of reed) are written on in ink. The Latin word for such a roll is volumen. *The Romans also wrote on wooden tablets.*

most famous poem is one about a pretty young woman called Lesbia who had a pet sparrow.

Virgil was the greatest of all the Roman poets. His most famous work is a long rhythmic poem called the *Aeneid*. This tells the story of Aeneas who escaped after the fall of Troy and found his way, after many adventures, to Italy, where he became the ancestor of the Latin kings.

Oratory – skill in public speaking – was highly prized by the Romans though, apart from Cicero's brilliant orations, few speeches were written down. Humour was also prized; Juvenal's satires poked savage fun at the fools he saw about him and Martial's epigrams were tiny gems of brevity and wit. Of the plays of Plautus and Terence, the favourites with Roman audiences were the most ribald and comic farces.

Roman writing materials (above): an ink-pot, pen, stylus, and wooden tablets. Hot wax was poured into the panels. When cool, it could be scratched by a stylus to write notes.

41

Law and Citizenship

Law is perhaps the greatest gift the Romans have passed on to us. The legal systems of most countries which used to be part of the Roman Empire are based on Roman law. (English law is an exception, being Anglo-Saxon in origin.) It was during the struggle by the plebeians to free themselves from patrician oppression that the laws were first written down. They were known as the Twelve Tables. Additions were made to them subsequently and points of law clarified.

As in England, the decisions of judges in the past were used to give guidance in fresh cases. The emperor Hadrian had these old decisions written down too. He also arranged for lawyers to be paid by the state, as before that they were unpaid.

At first only people living in Italy had full citizens' rights. Soldiers became citizens when they left the army, no matter where they were born, and worthy people in the provinces could also be granted citizenship. St Paul was a Roman citizen, which is why he was able to appeal to Caesar when accused by the Jews of causing trouble. Then in AD 212 a very important law was passed which gave Roman citizenship to all free men living in the Empire.

There were still large numbers of slaves, who had hardly any rights at all, though their masters could free them. After that they became citizens, and were often given important jobs because they were experienced in business affairs.

An orator in court. Much stress was laid on public speaking in a Roman boy's education, especially if he was marked out to be a lawyer or a senator.

Trade and Money

The peace the Romans brought to their Empire was a great help to trade. The Romans called the Mediterranean 'Our Sea' and merchants could sail around it without fear of pirates. They could also travel along the roads free from attack by bandits. The fact that the laws were the same in every place helped. Money, too, was the same wherever you went. Coins were minted in several different centres, including Lyons in France and Alexandria in Egypt, but the values were always the same, and a coin would be accepted anywhere, no matter where it had been struck.

'Struck' is the word we use for making coins, because straight after the blank coin had been cast in a mould it was placed in a metal die which had the design for the under side. Then the coin was hit with another die like a hammer, which had the design of the upper side on it.

The standard coin at the time of the Republic was called a denarius. Augustus issued new coins, the larger ones gold and silver, the smaller ones in brass, copper and bronze.

The Roman state depended on everyone paying taxes, and coins were used for this purpose. The

A selection of Roman coins. These coins commemorate famous men and events. The faces of consuls or emperors appear on one side, and symbolic scenes on the other.

This money changer is weighing coins in a balance. He would change large coins into small ones or small into large.

governors of provinces employed *publicani* to collect the tax money. Often both the governors and the publicani wanted to make themselves rich, so ordinary people were forced to hand over more than the official amount. The Roman Empire collapsed when there was no longer enough money to pay for the troops guarding the frontiers.

The Army and Navy

It was the army which made Rome a great power. During the Republic all soldiers were citizens, and men took pride in fighting for their country. Discipline was harsh. If a legion was thought cowardly, it was *decimated*; one man in every ten was executed. The Romans were victorious because they trained hard, learnt from their mistakes and never gave in.

As the Empire expanded, more and more soldiers came from the provinces. A legion, the Roman word for a regiment, consisted of about 5000 men, divided into cohorts and centuries. Each century (100 men) had its own captain, the centurion. The legion had a small number of cavalry to act as scouts and to guard the flanks. It might also have specialized foreign troops, such as archers or slingers, who were called auxiliaries. Legions were known by a number, such as the Tenth, plus a nick-name, like *Victrix*, which means Victorious. Each legion carried a standard made of bronze, with the symbolic Roman figure of an eagle on top. It was a terrible disgrace if enemies captured the Eagle.

The Roman navy was never as important or highly thought of as the army. Italy has few good natural harbours and the Italians were not seafarers like the Greeks. Nearly all Rome's sailors were foreigners. The Romans made their first fleet by copying captured Carthaginian ships. But it was their own idea to make beaked drawbridges called crows, which were dropped on to enemy ships so soldiers could cross over and fight. Warships had men pulling oars in two banks on each side. They also had a mast and sail, but these were put ashore before a battle.

Roman foot soldiers, shown in the background of this scene (above), were tough, well-disciplined professionals. Their weapons and armour were highly effective. Officers sometimes rode on horseback.

Soldiers in camp used to play dice (left) and board games like draughts to pass the time.

Weapons and Forts

If it was the army that made Rome great, it was the foot-soldier who made the army great. His special weapon was a short sword called a *gladius*. In battle he stabbed with it through the gap between his shield and that of the man next to him. Shields could be held overhead and linked together to make a solid protection, like the shell of a tortoise. His other weapon was a spear, over two metres long, which was hurled at the enemy when a battle started. A soldier on the march had to carry all his equipment, which weighed about 18 kilograms, and he was expected to cover at least 30 kilometres in a day.

A ballista (above) was a kind of catapult. It fired heavy bolts against enemy troops and fortifications.

48

Only the tents went on wagons, along with the camp kitchen, and the giant catapults called *ballistae* which fired heavy bolts and stones.

When an army was advancing into enemy country, it halted each day in the late afternoon and built a square fort. The soldiers dug ditches and piled the earth into a bank with a wooden palisade on top. The commanding officer's tent was in the middle, with straight lanes leading to it from the gates in the middle of each side, and the soldiers' tents arranged by centuries. Permanent forts were built of stone, laid out in the same way, with a shrine for the Eagle, weapon stores, granaries, a hospital and barracks where the soldiers lived.

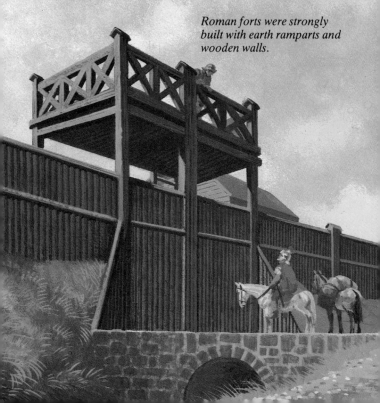

Roman forts were strongly built with earth ramparts and wooden walls.

Roads and Sea Routes

Many present day roads in Europe follow the lines of Roman ones. The Romans would never have been able to govern so vast an empire without their network of roads. By changing horses at the official posting station, a messenger could ride two hundred kilometres in a day. Troops could also march quickly to trouble spots. Roads were built by the legions as they advanced into new territory, the hard work being done by prisoners of war.

The Roman Empire was the largest the world had seen. It was held together by its roads and seaways. It was divided into provinces.

Britannia

Gallia (France)

Rome

Sardinia

Sicily

Hispania (Spain)

Carthage

Africa

Roman roads are not always straight. Sometimes they zigzag to get up hills, or bend to avoid mountains or marshes. Roads were paved only where there was stone close by. In other places they were built up with gravel to give a smooth surface.

The main roads linked up with vital sea routes. Six main roads led out of Rome. One led down to Ostia at the mouth of the River Tiber, which was the port for Rome. Merchant ships brought grain here from Egypt, metal from Spain and luxury goods such as silk and spices from the east.

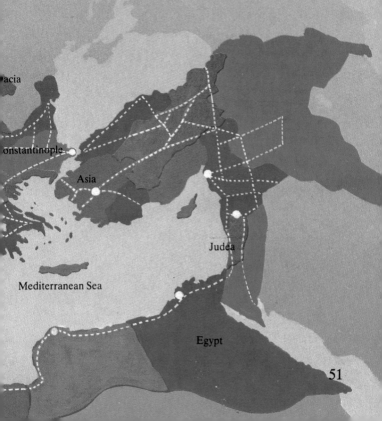

Dacia

Constantinople

Asia

Judea

Mediterranean Sea

Egypt

Ships of War and Peace

It has been said that free bread and circuses were all that the people of Rome needed to keep them happy. Corn for bread was brought to Ostia from Egypt in large merchant ships. The one in which St Paul was wrecked on Malta had 276 people on board, as well as its cargo. The captain of that ship had risked sailing late in the year. Normally all ships, merchant or naval, were hauled out of the water during the winter months. The harbour at Ostia was huge, with big warehouses all round. Goods were

towed up the Tiber to Rome in barges pulled by oxen. The Romans knew that moving heavy things by water was easier than on land, so where there were no rivers they dug canals.

In a sea battle the idea was to ram the enemy ship and sink it. That is why warships had spikes in front at water level. The fleet was mainly used for patrolling and for transporting troops.

A scene at a harbour mouth. On the left is a war galley with sailors pulling the oars. On the right is a merchant ship, steered by a large oar at the stern – rudders were still unknown. In between is a lighthouse to mark the harbour entrance.

Roman Emperors

When the Republic began to break down under the strain of ruling so vast an empire, ambitious men were ready to seize power – amongst them Julius Caesar, a wily patrician. The Senate appointed Caesar governor of Gaul (France), giving him command of a powerful army. With it he conquered the warlike Celtic tribes of France and Belgium, and even invaded southern England. Not content with this, he marched against Rome itself, crossing the Rubicon, a river which marks the boundary between Gaul and Italy. The Senate sent the great general Pompey to stop him, but Caesar defeated Pompey, first in Italy and then in Greece. Pompey fled to Egypt, pursued yet again by Caesar.

When Caesar arrived in Egypt he fell in love with Cleopatra, elder sister and rival of the young pharaoh Ptolemy. Pompey was murdered and so too was Ptolemy, enabling Cleopatra to become sole queen. She was worshipped as the goddess Isis in human form, and the Egyptians told Caesar he must be Amon, the chief god of the country.

Back in Rome, Caesar celebrated a triumph lasting four days, with feasting and gladiator shows. Though he was capable of just leadership, so much glory went to his head. He proclaimed himself dictator and it became clear that he even wanted to be king. So, anxious to restore the Republic, some senators stabbed him to death in 44 BC.

Julius Caesar wrote an account of the seven years he spent fighting in Gaul. He described events and people clearly and vividly. His book shows him to have been a skilful but ruthless general.

Augustus

After Caesar's death, people were surprised to learn that he had named his great-nephew Octavian as his heir. A more likely choice would have been Caesar's close friend Mark Antony, a brilliant general and popular hero, and indeed at first it was he who took power. He also took Cleopatra as his mistress, putting aside his wife (Octavian's sister). Octavian was only eighteen, but he was wise. Despite his youth and poor health, he defeated Antony in battle and became the first Emperor of Rome.

The Romans sacrificed animals in the hope of winning favour with the gods. Augustus took the old forms of religion very seriously and encouraged others to do the same.

Octavian did not abolish the Senate; he encouraged it, while making it clear he was master. He made himself head of the army, and so was called *Imperator*. The Senate gave him the titles *Princeps*, first citizen, and *Augustus*, which means worthy of reverence. His great achievement was in bringing peace and prosperity after the long period of civil war. He could be quite ruthless, but capable men were willing to work with him, and he was a great patron of artists and writers. He made the city of Rome much more magnificent than it had been before. He lived to the age of seventy-six, and died peacefully in AD 14.

Emperors, Good and Evil

The next four emperors were all related, if not directly, to Augustus. Tiberius tried to rule wisely but he had many enemies and was murdered. Caligula, a totally corrupt and probably mad despot, ruled for only four years before he was assassinated. He was followed by his uncle Claudius, who ruled wisely and well until AD 54 when he died, probably poisoned by his wife. Her son by a previous marriage, Nero, became emperor. This much-hated and dissolute tyrant is said to have set fire to buildings in Rome to clear a place for his palace. When the Senate declared him a public enemy he committed suicide.

Now there were no members of Augustus's family left and a struggle began among four rival generals and their armies. With the success of Vespasian came peace. He was succeeded by his son Titus, and then by Titus's brother Domitian, who killed many members of the Senate before he himself was killed. Nerva, the next emperor, ruled for only two years, and wisely adopted the successful general Trajan as his heir. Trajan, after two decades of peaceful rule, adopted his cousin Hadrian to succeed him.

Hadrian spent most of his time travelling round the empire to see that it was well governed. He even visited Britain and gave orders to build the defensive wall from Solway to Tyne which bears his name. He was a good administrator, and made governing the provinces a civil, not a military, job.

Hadrian built his Wall to keep wild Scottish tribesmen out of Roman Britannia. There were 17 forts spaced out along it and mile castles like this one at intervals of one Roman mile (1½ km).

Constantine

The return to peace accomplished during Trajan's and Hadrian's time did not last long. For a century and a half the Roman Empire was in turmoil. The emperor Diocletian brought stability, dividing the Empire into two with Rome as capital of the west and Byzantium of the east, and delegating much of his power. Though a capable ruler, Diocletian was ruthless and persecuted adherents of the expanding Christian religion.

In AD 306 Constantine, in Britain with his legion, was hailed as the new emperor. In AD 312 he marched on Rome and took command of the whole

Empire. A Christian himself, he gave Christians the legal right to practise their faith. Rome was being threatened by northern invaders, so he made Byzantium his main capital. He rebuilt it almost completely and changed its name to Constantinople. The whole of Europe and Asia was being overrun by tribes on the move. Rome fell to Alaric the Goth in AD 410, but the Eastern Empire survived for another thousand years, and produced the civilization we call Byzantine.

When Constantine reached Rome from Britain he had to fight a rival emperor. The two armies met at the Milvian Bridge near the city. It is said that during the battle Constantine saw a cross in the sky and heard a voice saying 'Conquer in this sign'. Constantine won the battle and large numbers of the opposing troops were drowned.

Index

Aeneas 41
Aeneid 41
Ahura Mazda 33
Alaric the Goth 61
Amon 54
Amphitheatres 14, 24
Amphorae 21
Ancestors 26, 34
Aqueducts 38, 39
Arch 38
Architecture 38, 39
Army 6, 20, 45–50
Arts 36, 37
Assembly, of plebeians 10
Augustus 20, 28, 31, 36, 44, 56, 57
Auxiliaries 46

Bacchus 33
Ballistae 48, 49
Bathing 22, 23
Beards 17, 61
Britain 28, 50, 58, 61
Bulla (lucky charm) 16
Burial 34, 35
Byzantium *see* Constantinople

Caesar *see* Julius Caesar
Caldarium 22
Caligula 28, 58
Capitoline hill 15
Carthage 13, 50
Carthaginians 7, 11–13
Catullus 40
Celtic tribes 7, 54
Central heating 19, 22
Chariot racing 25
Christianity 30, 31, 61
Cicero 41
Circus Maximus 15, 25
Citizens 20, 31, 35, 42, 46
City states, Greek 7
Claudius 28, 29, 58
Cleopatra 28, 54, 56
Clients 35

Clothes 16, 17
Coins 44, 45
Colosseum 14, 24
Concrete 38
Constantine 31, 60, 61
Constantinople 51, 61
Consuls 10, 11, 12
Cooking 18
Corn 21, 51, 52
Cremation 34
Crucifixion 31
Cybele 32

Dacia 37, 51
Denarius 44
Dictators 11, 54
Diocletian 61
Dionysus 33
Dome 38
Domitian 58

Eagle (symbolic) 26, 46, 49
Egypt 54; gods of 32, 33
Elephants 12
Empire 35, 56–61
Emperors 28, 29, 54–61; worship of 28, 29, 54
Etruscans 7–10, 32, 38

Fabius Cunctator 11
Farming 20, 21
Fashion 16, 17, 35
Fish paste 21
Flats 16, 18, 19
Food 18
Forts 22, 48, 49
Fortune 27
Forum Romanum 15
Frigidarium 22
Fruit 21
Funerals 34, 35

Galleys 24, 53
Gallic wars 54

Gaul 54
Gladiators 15, 24
Gladius 48
Gods 26–29, 32, 33
Golden House of Nero 38
Grammaticus 17
Greeks 6, 8, 17, 32, 36

Hadrian 42, 58, 59, 60
Hannibal 11–13
Hockey, Roman version of 24
Horace 40
Horatius 8
Houses 16–20
Hypocausts 22

Imperator 57
Industry 19
Isis 32, 33, 54
Italy 6, 12

Janus 27
Jesus Christ 31, 35
Jews 30
Judaea 31
Julius Caesar 12, 21, 28, 54–56
Juno 26
Jupiter 15, 26, 28
Juvenal 41

Kings 8, 10, 41, 54

Lares 27
Latin, language 7, 8, 17; people 7, 8
Law 42
Legions 46, 50, 61
Literature 40
Litterator 17
Livy 40

Malta 52
Mark Antony 56
Marriage 17
Mars 26
Martial 41
Meals 18

Mediterranean 6, 21, 44, 50, 51
Milvian Bridge, battle of 60, 61
Minerva 26
Minting 44
Mirmillo 24
Mithras 33
Money 44, 45
Mosaics 36

Navy 13, 46, 53
Nero 38, 58
Nerva 58
North Africa 13, 24, 51

Octavian *see* Augustus
Olive oil 17, 18, 22
Oratory 17, 41–43
Ostia 51, 52

Painting 36, 37
Papyrus 40
Pater familias 17
Patricians 10, 16, 17, 19, 35, 54
Paul, St 31, 42, 52
Pax Romana 31
Penates 27
Plautus 41
Plebeians 10, 42
Ploughs 21
Poetry 40
Pompeii 18, 37
Pompey 54
Pontifex Maximus 8
Pontius Pilate 31
Princeps 57
Priest 8
Provinces 46, 50, 61
Ptolemy 54
Publicani 45
Public baths 22, 23
Public buildings 14, 15

Querns 19

Religion 26–35, 56, 57, 60, 61
Remus 7, 8
Republic 8–12, 40, 46, 54

Retiarius 24
Rex see kings
Rhetor 17
Roads 14, 50, 51
Rome 6–8, 14, 15, 22, 38, 57, 58, 61
Romulus 7, 8
Rostra 15, 34
Rubicon 54

Saturnalia 26
Sculpture 37
Senate 10, 11, 13, 57, 58
Senators 10, 11, 36, 54
Ships 6, 13, 46, 52, 53
Sicily 7, 12
Sistrum 32
Slaves 16, 19–22, 31, 34, 42, 61
Soldiers 46–51
Sport 22–25
SPQR 11
Superstition 32, 33

Tacitus 40
Tarquinius Priscus 8
Tarquin the Proud 8, 10
Taxes 10, 45
Temples 11, 15, 26, 27, 38
Tepidarium 22
Terence 41
Tiber 6, 53
Tiberius 28, 31, 58
Titus 58
Togas 11, 16, 17, 35
Tombstones 35
Town, life in 18, 19
Trade 44
Trajan 37, 58
Tribunes 11
Triumphs 12–15, 54
Troy 41
Twelve Tables 42

Vault 38
Vegetables 21
Venus 27
Vespasian 58

Vesta 27
Vestal Virgins 27
Vesuvius 37
Veterans 21
Veto 11
Via Appia 50
Victory 27
Victrix 46
Villas 22
Vines 21
Virgil 20, 41

Water 19, 22, 38
Weapons 48, 49
Wine 21
Writing 41

Zama, battle of 12